START EXPLORING
MASTERPIECES

By Mary Martin
Stories by Steven Zorn

RUNNING PRESS
PHILADELPHIA · LONDON

20 19 18 17 16 15 14 13 12 11 10 9 8 7
Digit on the right indicates the number of this printing.

ISBN 10: 0-7624-0945-2
ISBN 13: 978-0-7624-0945-7

Cover design by Alicia Freile
Cover illustrations by Mary Martin
Interior design by Dennis Roberts
Typography: Berkeley Oldstyle by
Commcor Communications Corporation,
Philadelphia, Pennsylvania

This book may be ordered by mail
from the publisher.
Please add $2.50 for postage and handling.
But try your bookstore first!
Running Press Book Publishers
125 South Twenty-second Street
Philadelphia, Pennsylvania 19103–4399

START EXPLORING

MASTERPIECES

ARTISTS REPRESENTED
IN THIS BOOK

Audubon, John James

Blake, William

Bosch, Hieronymus

Botticelli, Sandro

Bruegel, Pieter, the Elder

Cassatt, Mary

Cézanne, Paul

Chagall, Marc

Chardin, Jean-Baptiste-Siméon

Charpentier, Constance-Marie

Daumier, Honoré

David, Jacques-Louis

Degas, Edgar

Delacroix, Eugène

Duchamp, Marcel

Dürer, Albrecht

Eyck, Jan van

Gainsborough, Thomas

Gauguin, Paul

Gogh, Vincent van

Goya

Greco, El

Hals, Frans

Hogarth, William

Holbein, Hans, the Younger

Ingres, Jean-Auguste-Dominique

Leonardo da Vinci

Manet, Édouard

Modigliani, Amadeo

Monet, Claude

Morisot, Berthe

Munch, Edvard

Piero Della Francesca

Raphael

Rembrandt van Rijn

Renoir, Pierre-Auguste

Rossetti, Dante Gabriel

Rousseau, Henri

Rubens, Peter Paul

Seurat, Georges-Pierre

Stuart, Gilbert

Titian

Toulouse-Lautrec, Henri

Velásquez, Diego

Vermeer, Jan

Whistler, James McNeil

CONTENTS

INTRODUCTION

CONGRATULATIONS! You're on your way to creating your own masterpieces.

The 60 illustrations of paintings in this book tell stories and legends, record events from history, and introduce you to important people of the past. Many of the artists who created these paintings weren't well-known during their own lifetimes, but today they're some of the world's most famous artists. Their works are seen by millions of people each year.

Be creative! There's no right or wrong way to use this book. Don't worry about neatness (unless you *want* to), and don't feel that you have to color within the lines. The artists who created the paintings shown in this book broke lots of rules on their way to becoming famous. They challenged people's ideas about how a picture is supposed to look. Who knows, someday your own original art work may be in a museum, too!

A word about technique—if you use felt pens or markers in your book, be sure to put a sheet of heavy paper or cardboard between the pages so the color doesn't bleed through.

Sleeping Gypsy

HENRI ROUSSEAU

(roo-SO)
Nationality: French
Style: Primitivism
Location: Museum of Modern Art, New York
Date: 1897

Henri Rousseau taught himself to paint, which may explain why his paintings look so different from anyone else's. His paintings have a dream-like quality, as though they take place in a world a little different from our own. Rousseau liked to paint jungles and wild animals, but the mood of these paintings is peaceful.

Rousseau didn't know that he was creating a new style of painting. He thought he was following the traditional rules of art, and he couldn't understand why his paintings were ignored by the important critics. But almost from the beginning, Rousseau was warmly welcomed by other painters.

Rousseau painted *The Sleeping Gypsy* as a tribute to his hometown of Laval, France, but when he offered it to the town, the mayor refused it. It is one of Rousseau's strangest paintings. There are only five objects in the picture: a woman, a lion, the moon, a mandolin, and a water pitcher. Each of these is familiar, but when you see them together, the effect is puzzling. The assortment of objects stirs your imagination.

Each part of this painting looks flat, as though it were cut out and pasted down, rather than painted. The woman looks like a paper doll. She still holds her walking stick, as if she were suddenly overcome by drowsiness. Her expression is peaceful and happy.

On the other hand, the lion looks startled, almost as if he's not sure how he got into this painting. His eye is wide and alert. His tail, like the woman's little finger, pokes straight out. The moon smiles down, bathing the scene in its silvery light.

This is a painting that shows us the imagination of an artist who tried to follow the rules of painting, but instead created a new way of seeing that others would try to follow.

The Syndics of the Drapers Guild

REMBRANDT VAN RIJN
Nationality: Dutch
Style: Dutch School
Location: Rijksmuseum, Amsterdam
Date: 1661

The human face was fascinating to Rembrandt. By looking into the eyes of one of his painted subjects, you can see what that person was like. Rembrandt also had a knack for capturing action. People in his paintings seem to be frozen in an instant of time.

A syndic is a businessman. The gentlemen in this painting are in the cloth business. It looks as though we're interrupting their meeting—each man is looking directly at us as if he's waiting for us to speak. Notice how the men are positioned. It's as if they weren't posing for a picture, but rather as if the artist surprised them.

The man on the right is handling a piece of cloth, the two men seated in the center are examining a sample book, and to the left, the man is just getting out of his chair. The look on each man's face is kind, welcoming.

A painting of a meeting of cloth merchants doesn't sound like it would be much to look at. But Rembrandt made *The Syndics of the Draper's Guild* hard to pass by, because he made you, the viewer, the center of the painting, and he filled each syndic's face with warmth.

The Dancing Class

EDGAR DEGAS

(day-GAH)
Nationality: French
Style: Impressionism
Location: Louvre, Paris
Date: 1874

No one is dancing in this painting of *The Dancing Class,* but there's a lot of movement going on. Notice how your eye sweeps across the painting, from the girl closest to you to the one in the far corner.

In most paintings, the artist wants us to notice a certain spot. *The Dancing Class* is different. Almost everything—the boards in the floor, the pillar in the corner, the huge doorway, even the dancers' elbows—point our attention around the room. Instead of one eye-catching subject, Degas has filled this dance studio with plenty of small details for us to discover. Did you notice the little dog? How about the girl trying to reach an itch on her back?

The Dancing Class is like a photograph taken by someone who was passing by. Nothing especially exciting is happening, but, as in a snapshot, every detail is recorded. Even though the girls' faces aren't clear, we can tell how the girls are feeling simply by noticing how they are standing or sitting.

The girl in the center of the painting is concentrating on the teacher as she takes a step. The girl behind her watches closely, her hand resting thoughtfully on her chin. You would expect to find a scene like that in any painting about dancers. But wait: not everyone in the studio is so intent on the lesson. Right above the teacher's staff you can see two young ladies who are more interested in their costumes than in the class. One toys with her tutu while the other picks at the bow in her hair. The girl standing in the corner braces her hands behind her neck as if she were tired of standing around. The three girls sitting behind the teacher are having a chat—and they probably aren't talking about dancing.

If Degas were painting *your* class, what would he see?

Maidservant Pouring Milk

JAN VERMEER
Nationality: Dutch
Style: Dutch School
Location: Rijksmuseum, Amsterdam
Date: 1657–1660

In 1866, a Frenchman named Joseph Burger saw a painting that changed the course of art history. The painting, *A View of Delft*, was a city scene painted nearly 200 years earlier by an unknown artist named Jan van der Meer.

Burger couldn't understand how such a masterly work could have been painted by an unknown artist. Surely, Burger reasoned, van der Meer's other paintings must have been credited to other artists. From that moment, Burger became a man with a mission: he scoured Europe hoping to find more paintings by this mysterious artist.

Burger's search uncovered 70 paintings by the artist, who is now called Vermeer. Burger wrote articles about the artist and sparked international interest in this forgotten master. Suddenly, Vermeers were turning up everywhere. But by 1907, experts agreed that only 36 paintings could be positively identified as Vermeer's work.

Vermeer's paintings are some of the rarest, most sought-after of art treasures. We know little about the man except that he was extraordinarily talented. He painted indoor scenes which usually show one or two women at a simple task, such as reading a letter, sewing, playing a musical instrument, or pouring milk. He usually showed a window to the left, with bright daylight dancing and bouncing off the figures.

The liveliness of Vermeer's light and the naturalness of his colors have never been equaled. Among the simple folds of an apron, Vermeer saw hundreds of shades of color, which he blended to duplicate the flowing effect of the fabric.

Art experts think that Vermeer used a simple type of projector to cast the image he painted onto a flat surface, much like a movie or slide is projected onto a screen. This flattened image made it easier for Vermeer to study the shine and sparkle of light on the subject he was painting. This clever technique doesn't make Vermeer less of a painter—his ability to capture these delicate effects on canvas make him an undisputed master.

Liberty Leading the People

EUGÈNE DELACROIX
(de-la-KRWA)
Nationality: French
Style: Romanticism
Location: Louvre, Paris
Date: 1830

Art books call this a "romantic painting." How can this be? A romantic painting doesn't necessarily show two people holding hands or kissing. A romantic painting can show almost any subject—even a battle. What makes a painting romantic is the feeling it tries to create—hope, imagination, or enthusiasm. Delacroix shows us these romantic ideals in this painting, which he called *Liberty Leading the People*. He was inspired by a real event that he saw—fighting in the streets of Paris during the July Revolution of 1830.

Delacroix came from a wealthy family and he sold his first important paintings when he was 24. He painted portraits, animals, and scenes from history and legends. *Liberty Leading the People* is the only canvas that Delacroix painted from his own experience. Although he didn't take part in the fighting, some people think that the young man in the top hat is Delacroix's self-portrait.

Liberty Leading the People combines the gruesome reality of battle with a powerful symbol. Liberty is shown in the form of a woman, similar to the Statue of Liberty in New York. Here she appears with the French flag in one hand and a gun in the other, fearlessly leading the people to freedom.

Look at the men around Liberty. Only a few of them are soldiers. The others are peasants, or gentlemen, or even boys. They carry whatever weapons they can find—swords, pistols, rifles—to help them in their fight for freedom. Liberty and her followers press ahead, unstoppable. A wounded man lifts his eyes for one last look at Liberty before she passes.

This is a painting about courage.

Starry Night

VINCENT VAN GOGH

(van-GO)
Nationality: Dutch
Style: Post-Impressionism
Location: Museum of Modern Art, New York
Date: 1889

When you look out your window on a starry night, you don't expect to see great swirls and whirls dancing in the sky. But that's exactly what Vincent van Gogh painted on a clear, quiet summer night in the south of France in 1889. Van Gogh didn't paint only what he saw in front of him; he also painted what he felt inside.

The dancing, shimmering lines of this painting tell you that this is a painting inspired by strong emotions. The stars swoop through the sky, overpowering the little village below.

When you add color to this picture, a different, tamer scene unfolds. Van Gogh loved color. He painted the planets cheerful orange and greenish-yellow against a purple-blue sky, creating a sense of joy and wonder. He painted the houses nestled at the foot of the mountains in deep purples and greens. The houses have their lights on, so it's easy to imagine people safe within. The twisting object in the front of the painting turns out to be a cypress tree, which van Gogh painted in curling lines of black and brown. Notice how the shape of the tree mirrors the church steeple.

Van Gogh had a short and sad life. He devoted himself to the appreciation of everyday beauty, but he was so eager to make others see it that he frightened people away. His paintings were not popular, and he suffered from fits of mental illness. He died in 1890, one year after he completed *Starry Night.*

The colors in *Starry Night,* which range from very bright in the sky to very dark on the ground, give order to the confused lines of the painting. Van Gogh shows us that even a tiny village has its place amid the great wonders of the universe.

The Vision after the Sermon

PAUL GAUGUIN
(go-GAN)
Nationality: French
Style: Post-Impressionism
Location: National Gallery of Scotland, Edinburgh
Date: 1888

The women in this painting are returning from church, where they have just heard an inspiring sermon. The sermon was given by the priest on the lower right side of the picture. It was about how Jacob wrestled with an angel to receive a blessing. It must have been a powerful sermon, because on their way home, the women share a vision of it.

Gauguin painted *The Vision after the Sermon* while living in a small village in France, where he began his career as a painter. Most of the people in this village were farmers and they were very religious. The women of the village wore the plain costumes you see in this picture.

The women in the painting don't seem surprised to be watching Jacob and the angel. Some sit calmly, as though they were watching a play. Others pray quietly. The priest, who looks a bit like Gauguin, bows his head.

Gauguin was experimenting with shapes and colors when he painted *The Vision after the Sermon*. He drew simple shapes which he surrounded with dark lines, like a stained-glass window. Instead of setting the action in the center of the painting, he pushed it to the upper right-hand corner and used the tree to separate it from the rest of the painting. The tree itself is a little peculiar; see how it lies across the canvas as though it has fallen. It acts as a barrier, separating the women from their unreal vision.

This is one of Gaugin's most important paintings because there is so much in it that no one thought of trying before.

Henry VIII

HANS HOLBEIN The Younger
Nationality: German
Style: German Portraiture
Location: Corsini Gallery, Rome
Date: 1539

Even if you came from another planet, you'd know that this is a picture of a mighty king. He's King Henry the Eighth, one of the most powerful rulers in British history. He sat on the throne of England more than 450 years ago, during a time of great political and religious change.

This painting is the most famous image of the king. King Henry must have been pleased by the likeness, because he hired Holbein to paint the rest of the royal family as well.

King Henry trusted the artist so much that he asked him to paint the portrait of a woman whom the king was considering marrying, but had never met. King Henry used the painting to decide whether the woman was worthy of becoming his wife.

This painting makes it easy to imagine how it must have felt to be king of England. The king's body fills almost every inch of space, calling attention to his dazzling, jewel-covered, fur-trimmed wardrobe. Even though the clothes are extraordinary, the king seems comfortable in them. He looks self-assured and confident—exactly the way a king should look.

ANNO ·ÆTATIS·   · SVÆ · XLLX ·

Luncheon on the Grass

ÉDOUARD MANET
(mah-NAY)
Nationality: French
Style: Realism
Location: Louvre, Paris
Date: 1863

The first time this painting was put on public display, the critics howled, the public laughed, and the emperor of France was shocked. If you think that all the fuss was on account of the nude woman in the painting, you're only half right. What also upset everyone was the two clothed men!

Artists had been painting nudes for hundreds of years before Manet painted *Luncheon on the Grass*. But the nudes in these older paintings were always goddesses, or historical figures, or else they were painted in dreamy-creamy ways that made them look unreal. Manet caused a stir because the nude in his painting is an ordinary woman, painted realistically.

Manet broke even more rules by including two men wearing clothes that were fashionable when the picture was painted. He made it clear that *Luncheon on the Grass* wasn't a scene out of history or from a legend. It was just a picture of a luncheon on the grass.

No one knew what to say about the painting because no artist had ever created anything quite like it before. To paint ordinary gentlemen in a natural setting was surprising enough. Then to add a nude woman to the scene was just too alarming for most people to accept.

Some artists did understand what Manet was doing. They agreed that artists should be free to paint whatever subjects they liked rather than repeating a few traditional subjects. These artists rallied around Manet and made him a leader of a new artistic movement.

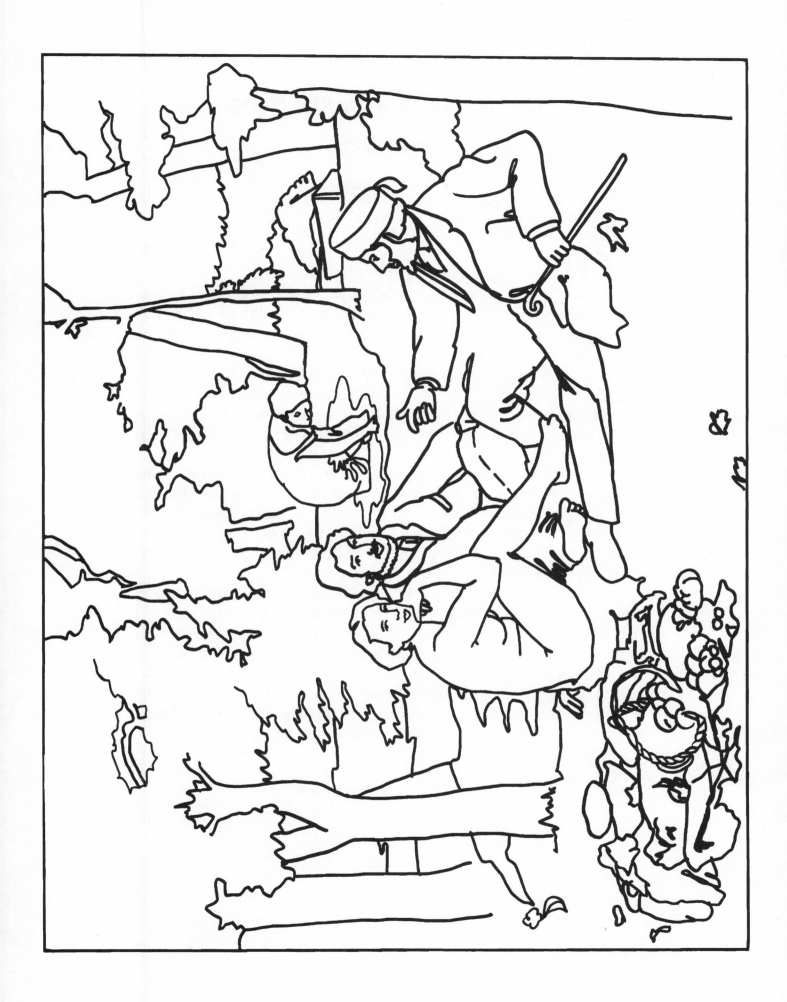

The Burial of Count Orgaz

EL GRECO
Nationality: Spanish
Style: Baroque
Location: Santo Tome, Toledo, Spain
Date: 1586

This painting tells the story of a miracle.

According to legend, a Spanish nobleman named Count Orgaz gave so much money to a local church that when he died, St. Stephen and St. Augustine came down from heaven to place the count's body in its tomb.

The Burial of Count Orgaz shows the two saints lifting the count's body. El Greco painted likenesses of Toledo's noblemen to witness the miracle. He also included a picture of his son in the lower left-hand corner, and some experts believe that one of the noblemen might be El Greco himself.

Above this earthly scene is a grand and dramatic view of heaven. El Greco captures the spiritual quality of the saints, angels, and cherubs.

The heavenly figures are drawn with bending, twisting lines that blend into one another. One angel carries Count Orgaz's soul, in the form of a baby, up to Jesus. The people on earth are drawn differently. They are lined up in an orderly manner.

El Greco's heaven is colored in rich golds and royal reds and blues. These colors shine against the deep black shadows and white highlights. For the earth, El Greco used very little color, except for rich gold in the fancy robes of the saints, which sets them apart from ordinary men. The priest's robe and the count's handsome black armor also have golden details. By using gold in this way, El Greco seems to be pointing out the holiness of the priest and the count—he's telling us that these two men are connected to both heaven and earth.

Jane Avril at the Jardin de Paris

HENRI TOULOUSE-LAUTREC
(tuh-LOOZ luh-TREK)
Nationality: French
Style: French Graphic Design
Location: various museums, libraries, and private collections
Date: 1893

Today, when we want to find out about the newest singers, we can turn on the TV and watch a music video. Even though these videos are made to advertise new talent and to encourage us to buy CDs and tapes, we can enjoy them as entertainment all by themselves.

In Paris in the 1880s and 1890s, before there was rock music, or videos, or even television, people went to music halls to be entertained. Most music halls used posters to advertise their shows. One hundred years later, the shows are forgotten, but some of their posters can still be appreciated. One poster that was created as an ad is Henri Toulouse-Lautrec's *Jane Avril at the Jardin de Paris.*

Toulouse-Lautrec was a painter, but he also created more than 30 posters. These advertisements were plastered on buildings throughout Paris and were seen by nearly everyone. Their clean lines, large, flat areas of color, and brisk design made them popular and eye-catching.

Toulouse-Lautrec's posters of Jane Avril helped to make her a major star of the dance halls. Today she's probably more famous than ever—not as a dancer, but as a subject of the great artist, Toulouse-Lautrec.

Third-Class Carriage

HONORÉ DAUMIER
(dome-YAY)
Nationality: French
Style: Naturalistic
Location: Metropolitan Museum of Art, New York
Date: 1860–1870

This picture of a third-class railway car was painted during a time when railroads were first being built throughout France.

Third-class was the cheapest way for people to ride— and also the least comfortable. The wooden benches were straight, hard, and close together, so people had to squeeze in. As you can see, it wasn't a cheerful way to travel.

It's not the crowd so much as the people in the front bench that Daumier wants us to look at. If Daumier had wanted us to feel crowded, he could have moved us closer to the people facing us. Instead, he gave us lots of room, allowing us to see almost their entire bodies.

The grandmother looks very old. Her face is tired and her skin is wrinkled. You wonder what she might have seen or done when she was younger. Next to her is her daughter, who looks healthy and strong. She's living a life of hard work, raising two children and looking after her mother. The children, meanwhile, are asleep. They are probably soothed by the chug-chug of the train engine. What do you suppose they're dreaming about, and where do you think they're going?

"The Mona Lisa"
(The Gioconda)

LEONARDO DA VINCI
Nationality: Italian
Style: Renaissance
Location: Louvre, Paris
Date: 1503–1506

Leonardo da Vinci was a genius. He was a painter, philosopher, scientist, and inventor. He invented the parachute in 1480, sketched a design for a submarine, and made detailed studies of human anatomy. He believed that sight was the most important of the senses and he carefully studied the world around him, keeping detailed notes of what he saw. Strangely enough, he wrote his notes backward, so that they must be held to a mirror to be read.

Leonardo wouldn't settle for a painting that was less than perfect. He would spend years working on a single painting, so he didn't produce many works. In fact, only 17 of his paintings have survived, and some of these are not finished.

Leonardo spent four years painting "The Mona Lisa." It's his most famous painting—in fact, it's the most famous painting in the world. You've probably seen "The Mona Lisa" before—in advertisements or on tee shirts.

No one is sure who the model for "The Mona Lisa" was. She's thought to have been the wife of a merchant named Francesco del Giocondo, so the painting is more correctly known as *The Gioconda.*

What's so special about "The Mona Lisa"? Many things. It's a skillful painting that demonstrates Leonardo's talent as an artist. It's also an almost eerie combination of a real-looking woman against a fairy-tale background. Especially, it's that mystic smile—a hint of a smile that's kept people talking for nearly 500 years.

If "The Mona Lisa" were the only painting that Leonardo painted, the artist would still be called a genius.

Saint-Lazare Train Station

CLAUDE MONET
(maw-NAY)
Nationality: French
Style: Impressionist
Location: Louvre, Paris
Date: 1877

In a world filled with beautiful things, why did Monet choose to paint a smoky, noisy, filthy train station? He painted this station about 10 times, and most people couldn't understand why he would bother. They thought such paintings were in bad taste.

In truth, Monet wasn't painting a train station – he was painting sunlight bouncing off the surfaces in the station. He was one of the first artists to take a serious look at how shapes and colors change according to lighting.

Monet realized that there's a giant step between what we see and what our mind tells us we see. For instance, at a train station, you may see a huge black box with steam pouring out the top. Your mind tells you instantly that it's a train, but if you think about it, it doesn't look like a train at all – it's just a black box of steam. You can easily recognize the train in Monet's painting, but if you were asked to draw a train, would you draw it the same way he did?

In addition to his series of train station paintings, Monet painted series of haystacks, water lilies, and buildings – studying them at different times of day, under different lighting conditions. He concentrated on the changing colors created by light rather than on the shapes of the subjects he painted. In his paintings, even solid stone buildings seem to be flickering images.

Before Monet, most artists made sketches outdoors, then went into the studio to paint. Monet made it popular for artists to set up their easels outdoors and paint what was in front of them. Monet's interest in light influenced an entire generation of painters – including Renoir, Degas, Seurat, and Cassatt.

I and the Village

MARC CHAGALL
Nationality: Russian
Style: Fantasy
Location: Museum of Modern Art, New York
Date: 1911

Like a dream or a memory, *I and the Village* is a jumble of images that overlap and fade into one another. A man and a cow stand almost nose-to-nose, a woman milks another cow, and around them are some topsy-turvy houses and people, and a plant. These seemingly unconnected, confusing images were taken from life in the village where Chagall grew up.

Chagall was born to a religious Jewish family in a small Russian city. When he was 23, he moved to Paris, where he painted some of his best-known works, including *I and the Village*. In this painting, Chagall looks back fondly on the village he had just left. The painting doesn't show the village in the usual way. Instead, *I and the Village* is more like the traditional stories of Jewish storytellers. A good storyteller can weave the simplest event into a tale so full of twists and turns that his listeners forget the reason behind the story. These tales become magical worlds of their own—delightful places to get lost in.

Chagall invites us into his world in *I and the Village*. The farm animals, the plant, the church, and the villagers flow together to create a single, solid picture of village life. The circular, curving lines seem to suggest the passage of time and the changing of the seasons.

Chagall was a modern artist, but he received his inspiration and his style from centuries of storytelling tradition.

The Washerwoman

HONORÉ DAUMIER
(dome-YAY)
Nationality: French
Style: Naturalistic
Location: Metropolitan Museum of Art, New York
Date: 1861–1863

Daumier wanted to be a famous painter, but people admired him only for his cartoons.

As a boy, Daumier had studied painting. When his father died, he had to find a job to support his family. He worked as a messenger for a lawyer and then as a bookseller. Both jobs brought him into contact with all kinds of people. Daumier would watch people as he worked, then go home and etch, paint, or sculpt them.

Daumier was very good at etching portraits and cartoons that made fun of people's behavior. Soon he was hired by a magazine to draw political cartoons. His cartoons were popular, but nasty. One of them made the king of France, Louis-Philippe, so angry that he sent Daumier to prison for two months. Upon his release, Daumier went right back to work and wasn't bothered again.

Between cartoons, Daumier painted as often as he could. His subjects were taken from everyday life – people in the theatre, people aboard trains, people at work. Unfortunately, no one paid any attention to these works until near the end of Daumier's life.

The Washerwoman is a good example of Daumier's painting. It's a simple scene without a story behind it. The sight of a young washerwoman with a small child and a huge bundle of laundry was common. Maybe that's why no one paid much attention to it. Daumier saw what most others failed to notice, and today this painting is appreciated for its simplicity.

Don Manuel Osorio de Zuniga

GOYA
Nationality: Spanish
Style: Classical
Location: Metropolitan Museum of Art, New York
Date: 1784

Something is about to happen in this painting.

What do you know about the boy in this picture? He's not standing in front of an interesting background, so you can't tell whether he's at home or in a studio. His clothes are simple but nice, so you know he's not poor, but neither is he royalty. He wears no expression on his face, and his pose is stiff and uncomfortable. You really can't tell much about the boy from this painting. But one thing's for certain—the look on his face will change the instant his cats pounce on his bird.

Goya arranged this painting to make it seem as though the boy is in control of his pets. On one side of the boy are caged birds, and on the other side is a bird on a string. But Goya shows us that the boy really isn't in control, because just behind him, his three cats stare wide-eyed at the bird. You know that in a minute, this calm scene will turn into mayhem. In a way, Goya left this painting unfinished—he set up the scene, but left it up to you to imagine what's about to happen.

Adam and Eve

TITIAN
(TISH-in)
Nationality: Italian
Style: Renaissance
Location: Prado, Madrid
Date: 1570

Have you ever done something you were told not to, and then gotten into trouble for it? Everyone has broken a rule at one time or another. That's one reason the story of Adam and Eve is the most popular story in the Bible. We've all felt ashamed of ourselves after disobeying a parent or teacher—so just imagine how Adam and Eve felt after disobeying God.

Titian painted Adam and Eve as they were just before the couple made their tragic mistake. The painting isn't exactly true to the Bible story, but it expresses the spirit of the story.

In the Bible, Adam wasn't watching when Eve plucked the apple from the tree of knowledge, but here we see him with a worried look on his face. He reaches out for Eve, perhaps asking her to reconsider. Eve isn't actually picking the apple from the tree. It's being handed to her by the chubby baby. Titian added the baby to show us that it wasn't Eve's idea to pick the apple. The snake, which persuaded Eve to break the rule, watches closely from a nearby branch.

The lush greenery of the Garden of Eden surrounds Adam and Eve. Two leafy branches cover their nakedness. Even though Adam and Eve weren't concerned about being naked until after they ate the apple, they were almost always painted standing behind leaves.

At Eve's feet is a fox, an animal that usually shies away from people. It's shown resting peacefully, a symbol of the innocence that will be shattered the moment Adam and Eve bite the apple.

Sunflowers

VINCENT VAN GOGH

(van-GO)
Nationality: Dutch
Style: Post-Impressionism
Location: Tate Gallery, London
Date: 1888

Vincent van Gogh worked as a preacher, a bookseller, a schoolteacher, and an art dealer, but none of these jobs satisfied him. When he was 27, he began to paint.

Van Gogh's first paintings were pictures of farmers and laborers in his native Holland. He used dark colors for these paintings, which gave them a feeling of sadness. No one bought a single painting.

Then van Gogh moved to the south of France, which was a sunnier, brighter place than Holland. Van Gogh began to choose vivid blue, bold red, and fiery orange and yellow paints. He daubed them onto his canvas in thick globs. Still, no one would buy his paintings; people thought they looked odd.

Sunflowers is one of the paintings that van Gogh painted in the south of France. Can you see why art dealers 100 years ago didn't like this painting? People expected a painting of a vase of flowers to be soft and light and peaceful. Not this one—van Gogh's sunflowers look almost as if they're on fire. Their stems and petals twist and curl, and the flowers look like they've been stuffed into the vase rather than arranged. Today, it's the naturalness of this painting that makes it so appealing. Van Gogh's quick brush strokes capture the simple beauty of the sunflowers. We wouldn't feel the same way about these flowers if van Gogh had chosen the most perfectly-formed blossoms and then arranged them carefully in an elegant vase. That would have emphasized the artist's skill; instead, van Gogh chose to show the crazy joyfulness of the flowers.

The Wedding Dance

PIETER BRUEGEL the Elder
(BROY-gel)
Nationality: Flemish
Style: Flemish School
Location: Institute of Art, Detroit
Date: 1566

You can see the wild merriment of a simple peasant wedding in this painting, and you can almost hear the noise as the whole village celebrates the happy event.

This picture is fun to look at because the longer you look, the more you notice. It's almost like a puzzle. How many people can you count? Can you find the bride and the bridegroom?

The bride is the long-haired woman just to the left of the center of the painting. She's the only woman not wearing a head covering. The man to her left is her new husband.

The artist painted this picture as though he were standing on a ladder, so we can see the whole crowd. If Bruegel had painted this picture from a ground level viewpoint, we'd be able to see only the people in front.

Bruegel painted many pictures of peasant life. These paintings may not seem unusual today, but they were startling when they were new, more than 400 years ago. Back then, life was difficult and short. Most art was created for churches or for rich buyers. Church leaders wanted religious paintings, and the wealthy didn't care much for paintings of peasants. But Bruegel appreciated the simple pleasures that the peasants sometimes enjoyed, and he captured those moments on his canvas.

Little is known about Bruegel's life. A biographer, writing about him several years after he died, wrote that Bruegel sometimes dressed as a peasant so that he could study village life without being noticed. Some art experts believe that he appears in *The Wedding Dance* as the man standing by himself on the right, near the musicians.

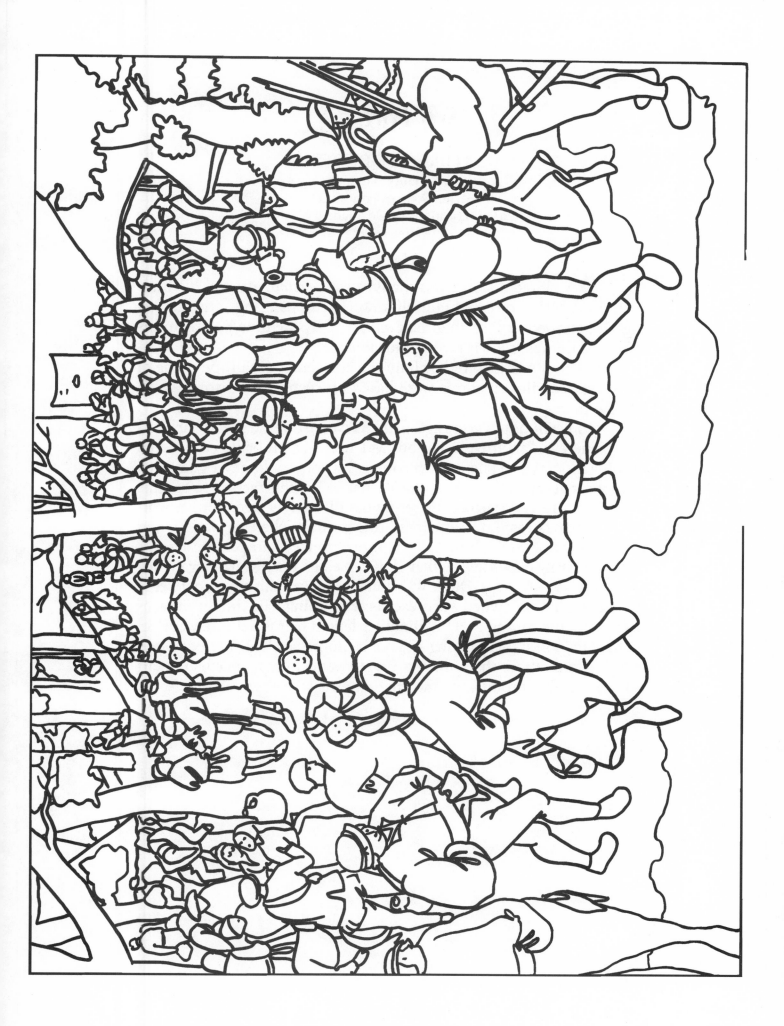

Self Portrait

ALBRECHT DÜRER
Nationality: German
Style: German Portraiture
Location: Prado, Madrid
Date: 1498

Albrecht Dürer was the greatest German artist of his time. He expressed himself in woodcuts, paintings, and engravings. He showed skill as an artist even at 13. By the time he was in his twenties, he was known throughout Europe.

Dürer was inspired by Italy, the arts center of Europe. Some of his most beautiful creations were based on scenery and works of art he saw there.

Five hundred years ago, painters weren't well respected in Germany, and even an artist as famous as Dürer was probably considered nothing more than a talented craftsman. But you would never guess that by looking at this self portrait – that's what makes this picture so special.

In his self portrait, Dürer paints himself as a gentleman worthy of anyone's respect. He painted this portrait when he was 27, and to look at him, you'd think he was more prince than painter. He sits regally, wearing expensive leather gloves, pleated linen shirt, elegant tasseled cap, and fine cape. Dürer was quite wealthy at this time, so it's easy to believe that he owned such exquisite clothing. His intelligent eyes peer out of the canvas, and his shoulder-length hair is delicately curled. It's hard to look at this painting and not be impressed by Dürer. But Dürer is trying to do more than impress us. He wants to convince us that art is a respectable profession, and that *all* artists deserve respect.

The Moulin Rouge

HENRI TOULOUSE-LAUTREC

(tuh-LOOZ luh-TREK)
Nationality: French
Style: Post-Impressionist
Location: Art Institute of Chicago
Date: 1892

Toulouse-Lautrec was born into an upper-class family, but his life wasn't easy. As a child, he broke both thighs, stunting his growth and leaving him almost crippled. When Toulouse-Lautrec grew up, he didn't feel comfortable with polite society, so he made new friends at the dance halls of Paris.

The Moulin Rouge was the name of one of Toulouse-Lautrec's favorite music halls. It's also the name of this painting, which gives you a peek inside the club.

The woman adjusting her hair in the mirrored wall was a featured dancer whose stage name was La Goulue. Her companion was also a dancer.

On the right-hand side of the painting, a curious woman is staring directly at us as she walks out of the picture. Toulouse-Lautrec showed her face as bright green in the hazy, harsh light of the bar, and he painted her lips bright red. The frills on her hat make her look like a big bug!

At the center of the painting is a group of friends enjoying drinks and chatter as they wait for the next show to begin. These people are regulars at the club. They're friends of Toulouse-Lautrec, and many of them appear in other paintings of his. You can see the artist walking by in the background with his tall cousin, Gabriel.

Through this painting, Toulouse-Lautrec captured the spirit of an ordinary night with friends at the Moulin Rouge.

The Birth of Venus

SANDRO BOTTICELLI
(bot-e-CHEL-ee)
Nationality: Italian
Style: Renaissance
Location: Uffizi Gallery, Florence
Date: 1485–1489

Italy was an exciting place 500 years ago, when *The Birth of Venus* was painted. People were examining the world around them through science and art. Christopher Columbus was planning to find a new sailing route to India, but instead would discover a new world. Inventions were being made, and new styles of painting and sculpture were being experimented with. One of the most famous artists of that time was Sandro Botticelli. Botticelli painted in the Sistine Chapel in Rome, and he had the support of the richest and most powerful family in Florence, the Medicis. *The Birth of Venus* was painted for one of the Medicis' homes.

Botticelli may have been the first artist to paint scenes from ancient Roman mythology. According to legend, Venus was the Roman goddess of love, and she was born from sea foam. Botticelli created his own version of the legend of the birth of Venus.

Botticelli wasn't trying to paint a realistic painting. The ocean is flat and looks like fish scales, the sky is a plain wash of gray, and the shoreline zigzags lazily into the distance. This is a fantasy landscape, the perfect place for a legend to come to life.

The goddess Venus is delicate and shy. Botticelli painted her skin a soft pink, like a rare pearl, and she seems to sway in the breeze blown from Zephyr, the god of gentle west winds. Clinging to Zephyr is Flora, the goddess of flowers. On the shore, a young woman steps forward with a cloth to cover Venus as she comes ashore.

This is a calm, relaxing painting, full of graceful, watery curves. The soft colors, the tumbling flowers, and the breeze-tossed hair and fabric create a feeling of gentle, dreamy motion. Here is a painting created purely as an object of beauty.

Rubens and His First Wife

PETER PAUL RUBENS
Nationality: Flemish
Style: Baroque
Location: Alte Pinakothek, Munich
Date: 1610

Shortly after he was married, Peter Paul Rubens painted this portrait of himself and his bride, Isabella Brant. Rubens was 32 and a famous, much sought-after painter. Brant was 18 and from one of the wealthiest families of Antwerp, Belgium. They were very much in love.

Rubens and his wife make a handsome couple as they sit among the honeysuckle vines. They look happy and confident in their splendid clothes. Isabella sits on an stool with her skirt fanned out around her. Her hand rests lightly on her husband's. Peter Paul sits up higher, his legs crossed and his thumb casually looped through the hilt of his sword.

This painting is full of curves and textures. Look how much of it is taken up by the twists and folds of Isabella's skirt and by the cape draped over Peter Paul's knee. These flowing lines are so different from the sharp, straight lines of Isabella's jacket and the pattern on Peter Paul's vest. Our eyes are treated to so many marvelous textures!

Even so, Rubens made sure that he and his wife didn't get swallowed up in all those lines. The couple's faces glow warmly against the darker background, and their clasped hands are the focus of our attention. Notice how their hands are in the center of the graceful curve of the couple's arms, and how Peter Paul's left index finger points to them. These joined hands are the most important part of this painting. They symbolize the joining of two lives.

The Bar at the Folies Bergère

ÉDOUARD MANET

(mah-NAY)
Nationality: French
Style: Impressionist
Location: Courtauld Collection, London
Date: 1881

Édouard Manet's father wanted him to be a lawyer, but eventually he allowed Édouard to attend art school instead. There's no doubt that this was the right thing to do. To become a successful lawyer, Édouard would have had to follow the rules of law precisely. Yet as an artist, he became famous by daring to break the rules of art.

Manet was one of the first artists to paint scenes from everyday life, rather than historical subjects. He believed that a painting didn't have to tell a story—that the purpose of painting is to experiment with colors and shapes. Manet's paintings were not understood by the art authorities of his time, and they were sometimes considered shocking.

The Bar at the Folies Bergère is one of Manet's last paintings. The Folies Bergère was the most fashionable nightclub in Paris. Manet's painting shows it to us in the mirror behind the barmaid. It seems like a grand place, with big chandeliers and lots of people. The barmaid stands in the center of the painting. Her face is blank, as though she's waiting for us to order.

At first, everything in this painting seems normal—until you notice that the barmaid's reflection is in the wrong place. Since we're looking directly at the barmaid, her reflection should be directly behind her. Instead, Manet painted it to her left and also added a man in a top hat who's talking to her. It certainly doesn't make sense.

The Bar at the Folies Bergère isn't what we expect to see when we look at a painting because Manet added his own ideas to the real scene he saw in front of him. Gradually, other artists started their own experiments based on Manet's ideas, and eventually earned the critics' respect. In this way, Manet changed art and the way people look at paintings.

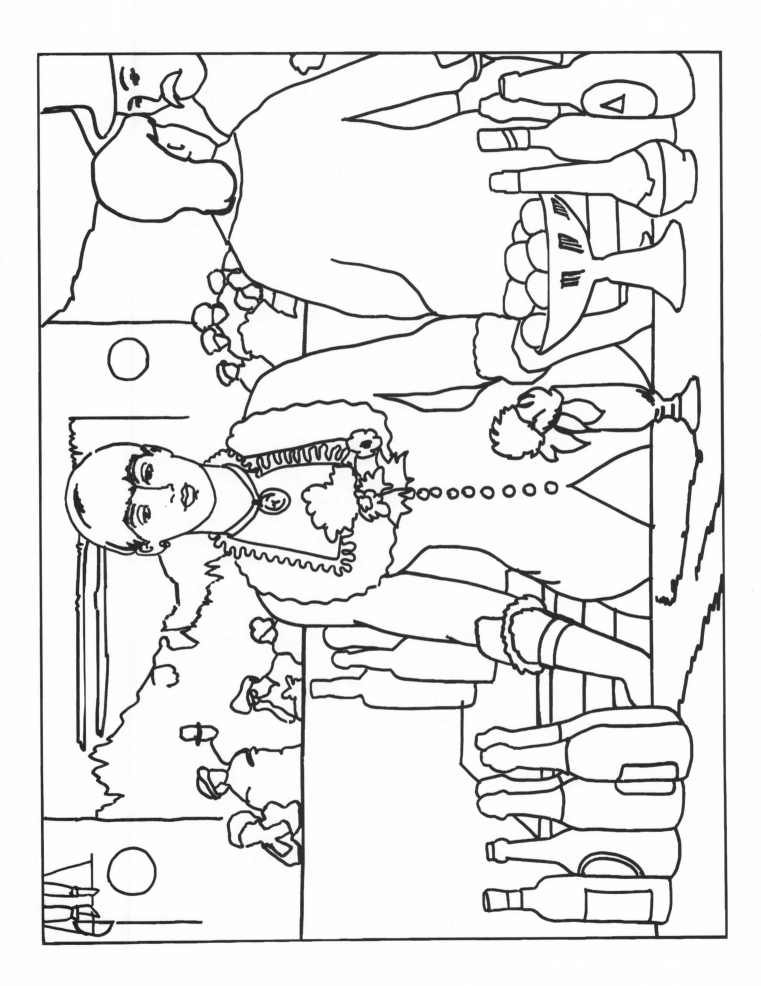

Luncheon of the Boating Party

PIERRE-AUGUSTE RENOIR

(ren-WAHR)
Nationality: French
Style: Impressionism
Location: Phillips Collection, Washington, D.C.
Date: 1881

Good food, good friends, and a beautiful day—have you ever seen a happier picture? It almost looks too good to be true. Look at how charming and graceful the women are, and how casual and friendly the men are. Everyone seems so relaxed. Their faces are half-smiles, their poses honest and natural.

Just as in real life, this large party is actually made up of several smaller groups of people. These smaller groups make the painting more personal. As your eye flits from face to face around the picture, you can imagine what each person might be saying.

Look at the three people in the upper right-hand corner. The two men are smiling as they good-naturedly tease the woman wearing the fancy hat and gloves. The woman, pretending to be shocked, puts her hands over her ears. Since she is so well-dressed, she probably came to the party with the man in the top hat. Most likely, they stopped by for a few minutes on their way to someplace else.

It's harder to figure out what the three people in front are discussing. One man is leaning over and looking at the woman. The woman is looking at the man with the hat, and he's staring into space. They don't seem to mind the woman who put her dog on the lunch table so she could look it in the eye and say cute things to it.

You might at first think that this painting is a jumble of people. Actually, Renoir constructed the painting very carefully. The poles that support the canopy divide the painting into easy-to-look-at segments. The railing also guides your eye as it cuts an imaginary line from the lower left all the way up to the man in the top hat. Most of the people are below this line.

You can imagine another line running from the center top of the painting toward the lower right, connecting the faces of the man talking to the gentlemen in the top hat, the woman taking a sip of her drink, and the woman looking at the man at the lower right. This imaginary line crosses the line made by the railing. Together the two lines form a triangle that our eyes follow without our being aware of it. Renoir planned his luncheon well!

Madonna of the Goldfinch

RAPHAEL
Nationality: Italian
Style: High Renaissance
Location: Uffizi Gallery, Florence
Date: 1506

A Madonna is a painting of Mary, the mother of Jesus. She's usually shown with the baby Jesus. Madonna paintings were painted to inspire faith in God through their beauty. Raphael painted several Madonnas for the homes of private citizens. He painted *Madonna of the Goldfinch* when he was in his 20s.

Madonna of the Goldfinch shows Mary, Jesus, and John the Baptist. The three are arranged in a pyramid shape, an arrangement that Raphael learned from studying the works of Leonardo da Vinci. The painting gets its name from the little bird that John is holding. The goldfinch is a symbol of Jesus because, according to legend, the bird got the red spot on its breast when it brushed against Jesus' crown of thorns. Since John was the patron saint of Florence, Italy, we can guess that *Madonna of the Goldfinch* was painted for someone living in that city.

Everything about this painting is peaceful. The sky is broad and bright, and the land rolls back into the mist. There's nothing here to pull our attention away from the Madonna and the holy children. Even the young trees in the background direct our attention to the main subject by framing the Madonna on two sides.

Raphael has made us feel close to the children by painting them as if he were sitting on the ground, at their level. He's also made them delightful to look at. John the Baptist kindly offers Jesus his bird to pet. Jesus, reaching for the bird, steps on his mother's toe. These details make *Madonna of the Goldfinch* an intimate, personal painting.

The Maids of Honor

DIEGO VELÁSQUEZ
Nationality: Spanish
Style: Baroque
Location: Prado, Madrid
Date: 1656

The artist is playing a trick in this painting of the young Spanish princess.

When he planned this painting, Velásquez was very clever. He could have painted an ordinary picture of the princess, her attendants, and other castle residents. But Velásquez painted himself into the picture, too: he's the artist on the left. By including himself in this painting, Velásquez created a picture of himself painting a picture of the princess's parents, King Philip and Queen Mariana. But where are the king and queen? They're standing outside the painting. In fact, it's almost as if *you're* the king and queen, watching Velásquez paint your portrait. This is a topsy-turvy painting–showing us not what the artist sees, but what the subject sees!

The Maids of Honor is even more curious because Velásquez thought of a way to include the king and queen in the painting after all. Can you find them? Look behind the princess. The king and queen are shown in a mirror behind the princess and the artist.

Even without this trick, *The Maids of Honor* is a skillful painting. Notice how the walls and ceiling draw your eye deep into the painting. Everything in the room is clear–from the dog up front to the man in the doorway at the rear. The scene looks real. You almost feel that you can step inside it and walk around, perhaps to peek at the artist's canvas.

"Portrait of the Artist's Mother"
(Arrangement in Gray and Black, No. 1)

JAMES McNEIL WHISTLER
Nationality: American
Style: American Portraiture
Location: Musée d'Orsay, Paris
Date: 1871

Most people call this painting "Whistler's Mother." The name Whistler gave it, *Arrangement in Gray and Black, No. 1,* isn't very catchy.

Whistler was born in Massachusetts but lived most of his life in England and France. He was a skilled craftsman who painted, made etchings, decorated room interiors, and even designed books. His paintings of London at night, his etchings of Venice, and his sense of humor made him a popular public figure.

Arrangement in Gray and Black, No. 1 is exactly what the title says it is—an arrangement of shades. Whistler chose black and shades of gray, but you could use blue and green, green and yellow, or any mix of colors at all. Whatever colors you choose, you can see how carefully the objects in this picture are arranged.

Pretend for a minute that Whistler's mother (her name was Anna) got up and left the picture. Is she gone? Good. Now you can see that the painting is made of perfectly straight lines running up and down and across. The scene is made of rectangles formed by the draperies, the paintings on the wall, the stripes on the floor, and the place where the floor meets the wall. Now bring Mrs. Whistler back. Notice how the tip of her nose lines up with the bottom of the picture frames. That makes the top of the painting look balanced.

We also have some curves in the picture now. The curves in Mrs. Whistler's dress, the lace of her hat, and her elbow all form graceful curves. In fact, Mrs. Whistler's whole body, from her head to her shoes, is one big curve. Notice how all the curves face in the same direction. Did you also notice the pattern in the draperies? That's right—more curves.

From this very simple painting, it's easy to see what a perfectionist Whistler was. His mother must have been proud.

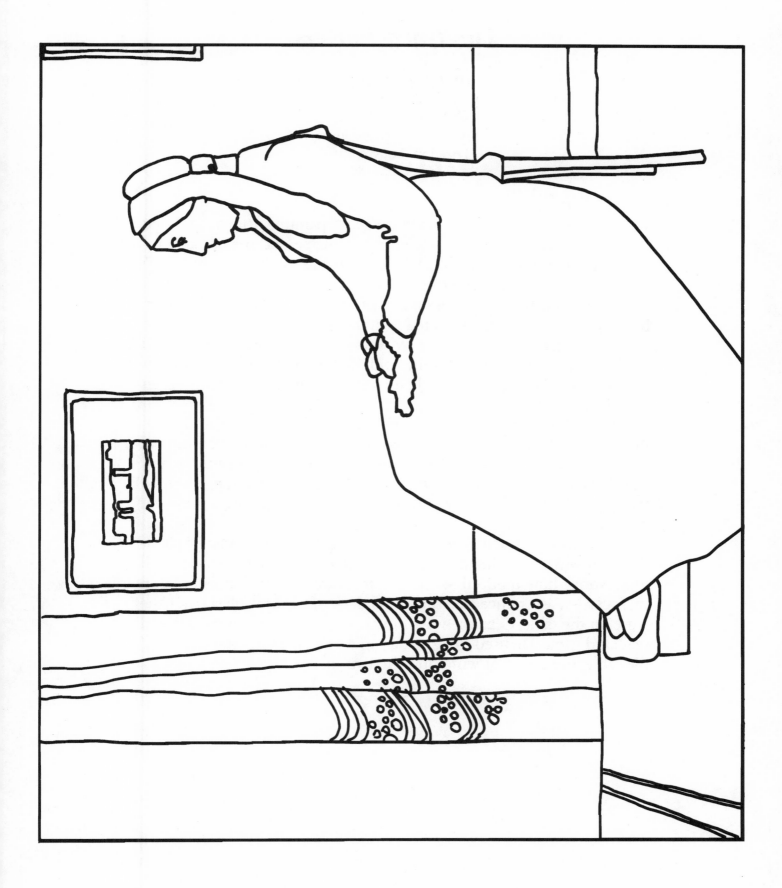

The Card Players

PAUL CÉZANNE
(say-ZAHN)
Nationality: French
Style: Post-Impressionism
Location: Louvre, Paris
Date: 1885–1890

It used to be easy to tell a "good" painting from a "bad" one. France was the art center of Europe, and the French critics made strict rules by which paintings were judged. If a painting didn't look a certain way, it was not considered art.

About 100 years ago, a group of adventurous men and women began to challenge long-accepted ideas about art. They began looking for new subjects to paint and new ways to paint them. While Manet painted scenes from everyday life, and Monet and Seurat experimented with ways to make painted light look real, Cézanne studied the shapes of objects.

Cézanne wished to make paintings that were "solid and durable, like the art in the museums," but he didn't want to rely on the old ways of painting. He wanted his paintings to make people aware of how shapes fit together or contrast with one another. In his paintings he tried to reduce the things he saw to their basic forms—spheres, cones, and cylinders.

Cézanne spent a lot of time arranging the subjects that he painted. Even when he painted people, he treated them as if they were still lifes. Notice how motionless the two men are as they concentrate on their cards. Also notice that there's no deck of cards or glasses for the wine on the table. Cézanne wasn't interested in painting a picture of a real card game. He used the game as an excuse to study the shapes of the table, the bottle of wine, and the two men.

The Artist in His Studio

JAN VERMEER
Nationality: Dutch
Style: Dutch School
Location: Kunsthistorisches Museum, Vienna
Date: about 1665

During World War II, this painting was owned by Adolf Hitler, the most hated man of the 20th century. He bought it for a museum he planned to open after he won the war. This painting and thousands of other art treasures were discovered in a salt mine in Austria at the end of the war, after Hitler's death.

Long before Hitler and World War II, Vermeer, who was broke when he died, willed this painting to his mother-in-law to help pay back some money he owed her. After that, the painting was lost for nearly 200 years, and when it turned up, it was credited to another artist. Eventually its identity was straightened out, and now, after changing hands many times, the painting hangs in Vienna.

The Artist in His Studio is one of Vermeer's last paintings. It shows an artist (possibly Vermeer) painting a picture of a model who's holding a trumpet in one hand and a book in the other. The model represents either fame or history. Behind her hangs a map of the Netherlands — Vermeer's birthplace, and a land famous for its arts.

This painting is filled with touches that make it unmistakably a Vermeer. The drapery in front of the painting, the table in the center, and the map in the background add depth to the work. Each of these items appeared in other paintings by the artist.

Rather than blocking off the room, the draperies force you to shift your attention more deeply into it. Your eye is stopped — just for a second — by the table and the artist's back. Then you look even deeper to study the model and the map.

Vermeer was so good at creating the illusion of depth that it's easy to forget that his paintings are nothing more than flat canvas covered with thin layers of paint. Here is an artist who could turn ordinary materials into breathtaking works of art.

The Merry Drinker

FRANS HALS
Nationality: Dutch
Style: Dutch School
Location: Rijksmuseum, Amsterdam
Date: 1628–1630

Frans Hals spent most of his life in Haarlem, a Dutch city springing back to life after winning independence from Spain in 1609. With his energetic brushstrokes, Hals painted robust faces beaming with national pride and the joy of living.

The Merry Drinker is a perfect example of Hals's works. The man in the painting is caught in action. His mouth is a half-smile and his right hand is gesturing as if he's saying, "Hey there! Glad to see you!" Notice how he's holding the glass—it's certainly not a very good grip. Perhaps someone just handed it to him. Or perhaps he's handing it to you. Whichever it is, you know that in an instant, his position will be completely changed. Hals's ability to "stop time" was a talent he shared with his countryman, Rembrandt, who lived at about the same time.

Hals painted about 240 works. Most of these are portraits of respected citizens; the rest are characters like *The Merry Drinker.* Unlike other artists of his day, Hals didn't sketch his subjects before painting them. He planned his paintings while they were in progress.

Hals's bold brushwork was another characteristic of his work. Most artists spent a great deal of time blending their paints to hide the brushstrokes of their finished paintings. Hals, on the other hand, made his strokes big and obvious.

Despite his uncommon style, Hals had steady work as a portrait painter. Yet even at the height of his career he had financial problems, and he died a poor man.

Hals's work was ignored by critics for 200 years. His lively brushstrokes were considered unprofessional and lazy. To the critics, Hals's paintings looked unfinished.

Then, in the 1800s, such painters as Monet and van Gogh rediscovered the excitement of Hals's work. Today, Hals is thought to be among the greatest portrait artists who ever lived.

Dancer with Bouquet, Curtsying

EDGAR DEGAS

(day-GAH)
Nationality: French
Style: Impressionism
Location: Louvre, Paris
Date: 1878

Edgar Degas studied to be a lawyer, but when he was 21, he decided that he wanted to paint instead. Luckily for him, his parents saw their son's talent and sent him to a good art school. It's lucky for us, too. Otherwise some of the world's favorite paintings might never have been painted.

In Paris, Degas studied the works of painters who lived hundreds of years earlier. These artists painted in a style that was seen as the "right way" to paint. The subjects of their works were almost always taken from history or ancient myths. (Botticelli and Holbein the Younger are two painters whom Degas studied. You can see their work in this book.) Degas, who wanted to make paintings he could sell, copied the style of these master painters.

But Paris at the end of the 1800s was a city where things were quickly changing. Degas saw a lot of new, fresh art that excited him. He began to develop his own style and to paint subjects that he enjoyed. Most of all, he enjoyed watching people. He liked to study how they moved as they did their jobs, and he painted many, many paintings of ballet dancers. In some paintings, the dancers are performing on stage; in others, they're in the dance studio, practicing.

Ballerinas were a perfect subject for Degas. They gave him a variety of postures to study, and because ballerinas are so attractive, Degas was able to sell his finished paintings.

Girl Arranging Her Hair

MARY CASSATT
Nationality: American
Style: Impressionism
Location: National Gallery of Art, Washington, D.C.
Date: 1886

Like the work of Degas and other French painters, *Girl Arranging Her Hair* captures a moment from everyday life. Here is an ordinary-looking teenager who's fresh out of bed. As she gathers her hair in a bundle, she's probably studying her reflection in a mirror and thinking, "Am I pretty?" or "How would I look in short hair?"

Mary Cassatt was born near Pittsburgh. She studied painting in the United States and Europe, and eventually settled in Paris. She made pastel drawings, oil paintings, and prints, which usually showed women and children playing or doing simple tasks. Her paintings were exhibited and respected in Paris, where she became friends with Edgar Degas and other young artists living there.

Cassatt painted *Girl Arranging Her Hair* to prove to Degas that she could create a painting that resembled Degas's own style. Degas was impressed with the painting and kept it until his death.

Cassatt's contribution to art wasn't limited to her paintings. She arranged a loan to a French art dealer who sold the paintings of Degas, Cézanne, Renoir, and others, but who was on the verge of bankruptcy. She also used her wealth and influence to promote these artists in the United States, giving them international recognition.

Cassatt was modest about her own work, and it is only recently that she has been recognized for the talented artist that she was.

The Ancient of Days

WILLIAM BLAKE
Nationality: English
Style: Romanticism
Location: Library of Congress, Washington, D.C.
Date: 1794

Some artists paint what they see. Others paint what they imagine. For William Blake, there was almost no difference between reality and imagination—what he imagined, he saw.

Blake was blessed with a powerful imagination. He declared that "only imagination is real," and that it is more important than anything else. All through his life he saw visions, and these visions became the subject of his writing and art.

Blake earned a living as an engraver, making illustrations for other people's writing. (His own writings and etchings were not well-liked.) He studied myths and literature from around the world, taught himself to speak five languages, and taught his wife how to read and draw. He invented his own printing process and made his own inks, and he began to make pictures of the myths he imagined.

The Ancient of Days is an image from Blake's complicated and wondrous mythology. In this picture, the god Urizen is planning the creation of the universe. For this job, he uses a giant compass, which had been a symbol of creation hundreds of years before Blake used it.

Behind Urizen is the fiery ball of the sun, and around him are dark, heavy clouds. The sun's brightness and the darkness of the clouds fight with one another. Over all, a strong wind blows, pulling on Urizen's long hair and beard.

The Ancient of Days isn't a painting. It's an etching, a type of black-and-white print. After it was printed, the artist colored it by hand—just as you can do.

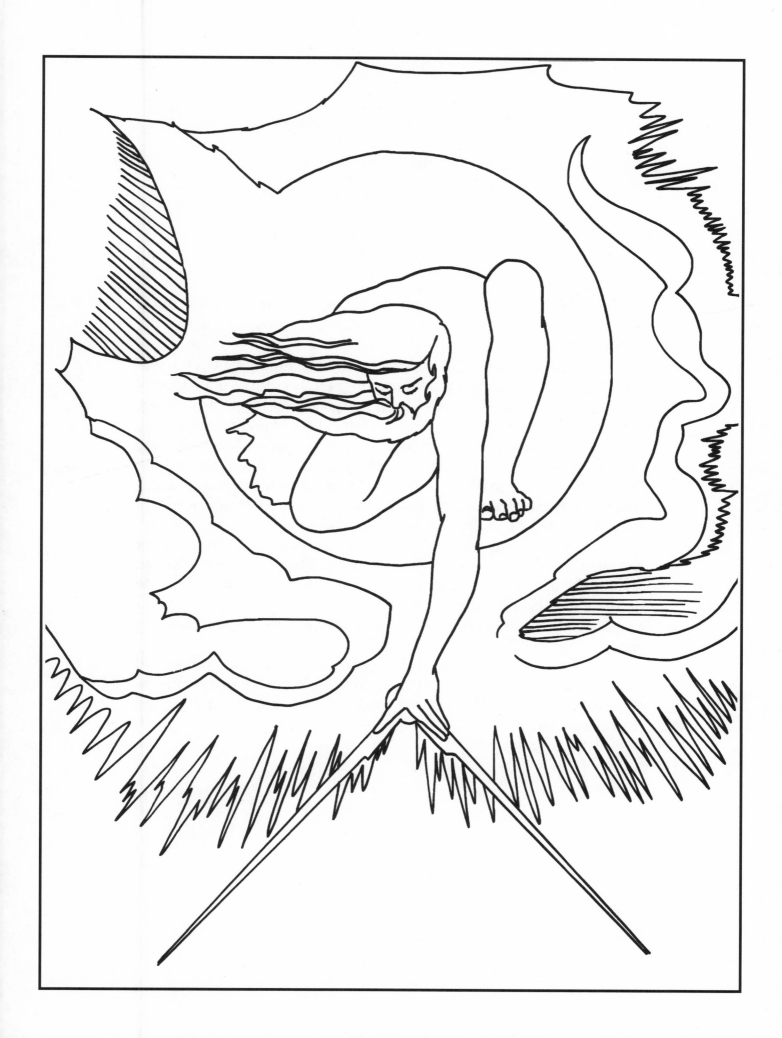

Hunters in the Snow

PIETER BRUEGEL the Elder
(BROY-gel)
Nationality: Flemish
Style: Flemish School
Location: Kunsthistorisches Museum, Vienna
Date: 1565

The name of this painting is *Hunters in the Snow*, but the hunters are only a small part of it. This is a painting about the icy quiet of winter.

Hunters in the Snow is one of a series of paintings about the seasons. Bruegel probably painted six paintings for this series—one for every two months—but only five have been found. Under a green winter sky, three tired hunters trudge through the snow. One of them carries a fox. Scrawny dogs follow them. You can see that it's the end of a long day for the hunters. This part of the painting, along with the inn and the fire-builders, would make a complete painting by itself. But Bruegel didn't stop there. He wanted to show more than the hard, bitter side of winter. He also wanted us to appreciate its magical side.

Down the mountainside, beneath the weary hunters, the river has overflowed and flooded the empty fields. The people of the village, making the most of the situation, have come outdoors to skate and slide on the icy patches. In the distance, even the sharp, rocky mountain is transformed into something delicate by a covering of snow and the fluffy dots of trees and shrubs.

To create this landscape, Bruegel combined images from several places that he visited. The mountains in this picture were probably inspired by the Italian Alps, but the vision of a late afternoon in winter is Bruegel's own.

The Oath of the Horatii

JACQUES-LOUIS DAVID
(da-VEED)
Nationality: French
Style: Neoclassicism
Location: Louvre, Paris
Date: 1785

Two hundred years ago, the people of France were growing angry because they had no voice in their government. The king and the nobility had all the rights and almost all the wealth, and many French citizens were starving. When the people could stand it no longer, they revolted against the king. They demanded liberty, equality, and brotherhood in a 10-year battle known as the French Revolution.

Jacques-Louis David took an active part in the revolution. He painted pictures of its heroes that captured the spirit of the times.

Many of David's artistic ideas were inspired by the art he saw while visiting the ruins of the ancient cities of Pompeii and Herculaneum in Italy. Among the ruins were pieces of pottery and sculpture that sparked new interest in the dramatic art of ancient Greece and Rome. This painting, *The Oath of the Horatii*, launched David's career. It is based on a Roman legend.

According to the legend, the Horatius brothers of Rome agreed to fight the Curiatius brothers of Alba to decide whose city was the greatest. It was to be a fight to the death. The brothers are shown pledging their loyalty to their father before they go into battle.

The women at the right are the Horatius sisters. One of the sisters is in love with one of the Curiatii. She knows that if her brothers win, her lover will die; but if her lover wins, she'll lose her brothers. For her there will be no happy ending. All of the sisters are terribly upset by the situation.

The powerful realism of the sisters' despair beside the brothers' vigorous heroism made David a hero among the artists who studied his work and who were inspired to paint in this dramatic style.

Mlle. Charlotte du Val d'Ognes

CONSTANCE-MARIE CHARPENTIER
(shar-pahn-TYAY)
Nationality: French
Style: French Academic
Location: Metropolitan Museum of Art, New York
Date: around 1800

Once, women weren't brought up to be artists. Even women who painted weren't considered artists—they were thought to be hobbyists. It was considered unladylike for a woman to be a good painter.

A woman who truly wanted to paint faced many difficulties. She would probably have to teach herself to paint, since she wouldn't be allowed to attend art classes. Most well-known early female artists were the daughters, nieces, or sisters of famous male artists. Having an artist in the family was often the only way that a woman could get professional training and a supply of paints.

In the late 1700s, French art schools began opening their doors to women, and talented women artists were able to take lessons from famous male painters. Constance-Marie Charpentier was one such talented woman. Her most famous teacher was Jacques-Louis David.

Like her teacher, Charpentier painted portraits as well as scenes of mythological figures. When she showed her paintings at major exhibitions, she won awards. Today, most of her paintings are lost or forgotten.

Mlle. Charlotte du Val d'Ognes was one of Charpentier's "lost" paintings—even though it has been hanging in the Metropolitan Museum in New York since 1922. You see, this painting was thought to be painted by none other than David, not by one of his students. Charpentier was credited with painting it when old records showed that the painting had been displayed at a French exhibition in which David did not participate. David's name was removed from the frame in 1977.

The mistaken identity of this painting makes it tempting to wonder how many other masterpieces might be credited to the wrong artist.

Lady Lilith

DANTE GABRIEL ROSSETTI
Nationality: English
Style: Pre-Raphaelite
Location: Metropolitan Museum of Art, New York
Date: 1867

The beautiful Lady Lilith is actually a demon.

In ancient Jewish folklore, Lilith was Adam's first wife, created at the same time as Adam. Despite her beauty, Lilith was evil, and she gave birth to demons. When she fled the Garden of Eden, God sent three angels to bring her back, but they were unsuccessful. For a long time, superstitious people believed that lovely Lilith roamed the earth creating more demons. To protect themselves from these monsters, people who believed the story wore charms with the names of the three angels.

Rossetti earned a living as a painter, but he was also a poet. He read widely and based his poems and his paintings on famous religious and mythological themes. He painted many pictures of legendary women. He married his favorite model, but she was in poor health and died soon after.

Rossetti painted *Lady Lilith* five years after his wife's death. The model was Rossetti's girl friend, Fanny Cornforth.

To look at Lilith, you would never guess that she is a monster. She looks like a picture of feminine grace, wearing a flowing white gown and surrounded by delicate flowers. But that's where the danger lies. Lilith is a woman whom men can't resist. She combs her fiery mane of hair, totally aware of her witch's power. As she gazes at herself in the mirror, what evil thoughts are going through her mind?

The Queen of Sheba (detail)

PIERO DELLA FRANCESCA
(PYER-o DAY-la fran-CHAY-ska)
Nationality: Italian
Style: Renaissance
Location: Church of San Francesco, Arezzo, Italy
Date: 1452–1466

A Christian legend says that when Adam died, his son Seth planted seeds from the tree of life in his throat. From these seeds grew a tree that eventually provided the wood for Jesus' cross.

Like all legends, the legend of the true cross is full of turns and twists, making it a fascinating story. Piero Della Francesca painted pictures of the important parts of the legend on the walls of the Church of San Francesco in Italy. *The Battle of Constantine* on page 50 is another painting from this series.

When painting on walls, artists sometimes use a technique called "fresco." To make a fresco, an artist grinds colors into a powder, mixes them with water, and brushes them onto plaster before it sets. Although Piero's frescos are damaged in spots, it's still easy to see the stories they tell, more than 500 years after they were painted.

According to legend, King Solomon cut down Adam's tree to use in his temple, but instead the wood was made into a bridge. In the detail of the painting shown here, the Queen of Sheba first sees the bridge and recognizes the holy wood. Earlier, she had dreamed that this piece of wood was to become the cross of Jesus. She told King Solomon that if the wood were made into a cross, it would be bad for his people.

King Solomon had the bridge taken down and buried, but eventually a pool was built over it and the wood floated to the surface, where it was found and made into the cross.

Back from the Market

JEAN-BAPTISTE-SIMÉON CHARDIN
(shar-DAHN)
Nationality: French
Style: Naturalism
Location: Louvre, Paris
Date: 1739

Who would want a painting of a woman returning home with the groceries?

Lots of people!

Chardin's simple subjects appealed to kings and commoners— at least for a while.

Chardin was the son of a Paris cabinetmaker. He lived a simple life, never traveling far from his native city. Chardin considered himself to be a craftsman like his father, rather than an artist. Although he trained with other artists, he never took a formal art course.

Success came early to Chardin. His first paintings were still lifes— paintings of ordinary objects in everyday settings. When he was 29, he showed his paintings for the first time. They were well-liked, and Chardin was invited to join the French Royal Academy, which was a great honor.

As his popularity increased, Chardin began to paint pictures of people. Even though his choice of subjects changed, Chardin didn't lose his simple style. The people he painted were maids and housewives and children. The pictures sold well. Some of them were so popular that he sometimes had to paint several copies to satisfy his customers! Even the king of France accepted two of Chardin's paintings.

But people's tastes change. Toward the end of Chardin's career, the public lost interest in his work, and he had a difficult time selling his paintings.

He died almost forgotten, but today we recognize Chardin as a great painter who had the talent to create art out of everyday life.

Erasmus of Rotterdam

HANS HOLBEIN the Younger
Nationality: German
Style: German Portraiture
Location: Louvre, Paris
Date: 1523

Hans Holbein the Younger was the most talented member of a family of artists. He created book illustrations, stained glass, and wall murals, but he's best known for his portraits of famous people.

In 1515, Holbein was working for a publisher, and he drew illustrations for a book written by Erasmus of Rotterdam, a well-known philosopher and scholar. Later, the two men met, and eventually Holbein painted three portraits of Erasmus.

Like most of Holbein's portraits, this portrait of Erasmus is very simple. Holbein was an expert at capturing a person's likeness and personality without adding many details. He painted exactly what he saw, and he didn't try to make a person look more attractive than that person actually was. This was the secret of Holbein's success: he lived in politically troubled times, but because he didn't take sides, his paintings were in demand by everyone.

Holbein always tried to paint his subjects while they were working or surrounded by the tools of their trade. In this way, Holbein painted not only people's likenesses, but also their roles in society.

The sheet of paper and the pen tell us right away that this is a painting of a scholar. Erasmus wasn't a handsome man, but his face shows character and wisdom. To look at this painting of Erasmus is to see the honesty of Holbein's work.

Gypsy Woman with Baby

AMADEO MODIGLIANI
(mo-del-YA-nee)
Nationality: Italian
Style: Primitivism
Location: Chester Dale Collection, New York
Date: 1916

Look closely at this woman and you'll see that nothing about her seems real. Her face is too oval, her neck and body are much too long, and her fingers are a jumbled zigzag. But still, you can't deny that this is a picture of a woman.

Even though the woman in this portrait is drawn with distorted lines, she's still very human. Modigliani learned this style from studying African art. Using simple lines and shapes, Modigliani was able to paint a portrait that catches our interest. The woman's long, narrow body—and especially her face and neck—make the gypsy seem elegant and regal.

Notice how flat she looks. Even though she's seated, she looks as if she's standing. Our only clues are the slight flaring of her skirt where her bent knees would be, and part of a chair poking above her right shoulder.

Modigliani painted many portraits in this simple, primitive style. Oval heads, big eyes, and tiny mouths are features of almost all of his works. Yet each painting is different from the others. Each captures something personal about the subject. Don't you get the feeling that if you saw this gypsy woman walking down the street, you'd recognize her?

Nude Descending a Staircase, No. 2

MARCEL DUCHAMP
(doo-SHAM)
Nationality: French
Style: Cubism
Location: Museum of Art, Philadelphia
Date: 1912

This painting is so outrageous that even the most open-minded modern artists of its time disliked it. Strangely enough, today it's considered one of Duchamp's tamer works of art.

In *Nude Descending a Staircase,* Duchamp combined ideas of two schools of art that couldn't agree on what art should look like. One group said that art should express speed and motion, as machines do. These artists called themselves "futurists." The other group of artists, the "cubists," thought that more attention should be paid to an object's shape. Duchamp used the blocky shapes of the cubists to paint a body in motion. It caused a scandal! When Duchamp submitted this painting to an exhibition of modern art, his brothers, who were on the selection committee, rejected it!

The painting was displayed shortly afterward in the 1913 New York Armory Show, the first major exhibit of modern art in the United States. Curiosity-seekers turned out to look at the odd creations known as modern art. The painting singled out time and again was *Nude Descending a Staircase.* It made Duchamp a celebrity.

The idea for *Nude Descending a Staircase* was probably inspired by early photographs of people in motion. Can you see the nude in this painting? She appears not once, but several times. The arms, legs, and head overlap themselves and blend, mimicking the effect of motion. If you concentrate, you can see the roundness of the head, the bent arm, and the long legs.

Duchamp made only a few more paintings after this one, and then he began producing objects that were not quite sculptures, but not exactly paintings, either. He wanted to shake up the whole idea of what art could be. His most surprising idea was that ordinary objects can be called art. His "ready-made" art includes a bicycle wheel mounted on a stool, and a bird cage filled with small cubes of marble and a thermometer.

Considered peculiar at first, Duchamp's objects are now at home in some of the world's most important art museums. Duchamp's creative way of seeing made modern art truly modern.

The Shrimp Girl

WILLIAM HOGARTH
Nationality: English
Style: English School
Location: National Gallery, London
Date: around 1750

Before William Hogarth, English art critics ignored English painters. They believed that fine art came from other countries.

Hogarth began his artistic career at the age of 15, as a silver engraver. Later, he took a few painting classes, but mostly he taught himself to paint. He chose to paint from life rather than from models in classes.

Hogarth dreamed of painting historical subjects. He admired the work of a painter named Sir James Thornhill and was lucky enough to be able to study under him. Hogarth fell in love with Thornhill's daughter, Jane, but Thornhill disapproved of the relationship. The couple eloped, breaking the friendship between Hogarth and Thornhill. Shortly after the marriage, Hogarth became a successful portrait painter and earned back Thornhill's respect and friendship.

Soon bored by portrait painting, Hogarth decided to paint humorous pictures that made fun of English life, especially in the city. From each of these paintings, he engraved a series of inexpensive prints which he sold to a wide audience. These prints were tremendously successful, and today Hogarth is remembered mainly for these pictures. Hogarth also was responsible for producing the first public exhibition of contemporary English art.

To protect his work from being copied by other artists, Hogarth fought for a copyright law, passed in 1735, which became known in England as The Hogarth Act.

Near the end of his career, Hogarth painted *The Shrimp Girl*. He combined his skill as a portraitist with his love of London street life to paint a picture of a young woman who sells shrimp. The woman has a warm smile on her lips and a rosy blush to her cheeks. It's a casual painting that Hogarth painted for his own pleasure.

Giovanni Arnolfini and His Wife

JAN VAN EYCK
Nationality: Flemish
Style: Flemish School
Location: National Gallery, London
Date: 1434

Most married couples put away their marriage certificate in a desk drawer or a safety deposit box. But Mr. and Mrs. Arnolfini hung theirs on a wall—and now it's in the National Gallery in London!

This splendid wedding picture, *Giovanni Arnolfini and His Wife,* is also an extravagant legal document. Like the marriage certificates that couples get today, this painting could be used to prove that the couple was married. It's even signed by a witness—above the round mirror are the words meaning "Jan van Eyck was here." (Although you can't see it in this drawing, the actual painting shows a tiny image of van Eyck and another witness reflected in the mirror.)

Experts once thought that van Eyck invented the technique of oil painting, but it's more likely that he perfected it. He painted thin glazes over heavy colors to create a rich luster that's lasted for more than 500 years. Van Eyck was also among the first to paint realistic pictures of people in their homes.

The Arnolfinis picked a good day to get married. The sun is shining through the window, brightening everything in the room. In the candelabrum, a single candle is burning, symbolizing the eye of God watching the ceremony.

Mr. and Mrs. Arnolfini are barefoot. Mrs. Arnolfini has left her shoes at the back of the room, and Mr. Arnolfini's shoes are in front. Their bare feet could symbolize their wish for comfort in the marriage and at home. They might also mean that the couple is standing on holy ground. The dog, besides making the picture feel casual, also symbolizes faithfulness in the marriage.

Marriage ceremonies have changed a lot since Giovanni Arnolfini and his wife were wed. Isn't it lucky that van Eyck invited us to witness this wedding with him?